SHADOW WORK JOURNAL

SHADOW WORK

With shadow work, you will find yourself being compelled to confront a lot of dark things from your past. Things that you probably put away in mental boxes, sealed with duct tape, and kept hidden in the darkest corners of your mind. This can be very unpleasant, uncomfortable, and sometimes even draw up a well of pain that you've been trying to escape.

So how on earth could shadow work possibly be beneficial to you as a Black man when it'll probably provoke a ton of tears and bring back unwanted memories?

Well, that's the thing about shadow work. The benefits lie in the challenges that it establishes. It's simply like an obstacle course. The wins lie at the end of the course. But you have to jump every hurdle, scale every wall, and crawl through every low to earn those wins.

Shadow work enables you to discover and accept the authentic you. As Black man, this is extremely important because many of us have struggled for long with our identities. Shadow work therapy will help you to prevail against that struggle. Accepting your identity fully not only improves your own wellness and mental health but also makes you open to accepting others for who they are as well. Finally, the practice of shadow work may not be easy, but the ends make it totally worth it.

SELF-GROWTH & SELF-IMPROVEMENT

Growth is all about stepping out of the old and into the new and the better. However, it might be impossible to discover the new and better you if you don't know who you are right now as well as who you've been in the past.

If you do not confront the parts of yourself that you've hidden (for any reason at all), those "shadows" will always come back to haunt you. They may even cause you to remain stagnant, unable to encounter your future because your past is holding you back. Your shadows can cause you self-doubt, make you scared to go for what you want, mentally enslave you and make you underproductive, and generally hinder you from becoming your best self.

Thus, the intervention of shadow work will enable you to break through all these barriers to your self-growth and self-improvement. Self-improvement for Black men is so important, especially today. We're now able to reach for heights that we could've only dreamed of attaining in the past. High-quality education. Jobs that we couldn't get hired into before owing to racism. Political positions. Winning prestigious awards and honorable recognitions. Inventing and innovating ideas and technology that revolutionize the world.

There's so much that Black men are capable of in the society of today. Therefore, to realize our greatness, we must weaken the hold that our shadows have on us. And this is where shadow work can help.

HEALING JOURNEY

When you've experienced deep pain and hurt—whether physical, mental, or emotional—you often get different therapies and rehabilitation methods recommended to you. Most of these therapies thrust you right into how to move on and look into a brighter future. Unfortunately, that's not the best way to begin healing.

To effectively heal from anything—could be trauma, rejection, depression, a broken heart, disappointment, grief, or failure—you must begin by addressing your pain. It has been statistically proven that Black men experience more trauma at a disproportionate rate to other individuals. So in order to begin true healing, you must confront and acknowledge these traumas first.

We'd also like to state that whatever you may have been through or experienced in life, you're not a victim. You're a survivor. So as you reacquaint yourself with your pain and your "shadows" and begin your journey towards healing, you should keep in mind that those shadows don't completely define you. Once you begin to experience genuine healing, you will discover all over again how strong you really are as a Black man.

A special aspect of this benefit is the part that has to do with healing from generational trauma. This has to do with healing from very early wounds, often inflicted or caused by primary caregivers like a parent. This is especially important so that the lineage of generational trauma can end with you and you don't end up passing it on to your own children.

AUTHENTICITY

Shadow work forces you to confront the real you, not just the you that the world finds acceptable.

As you know, your "shadows" are the sides of yourself that hold your repressed traumas, humiliations, guilts, and all the parts of yourself that you've sought to hide not just from others but also from yourself. Shadow work brings these shadows to light, and by doing this, stops you from being in denial of who you truly are.

Again, your shadows don't completely define you. They may be truths about your life and your past, but they're not what makes you authentic. What makes you authentic is the fact that you're a man who has faced his fears, faced his pain, and discovered how strong and truly better he can become for it.

Shadow work makes you own up to your past and build a brighter future for yourself on a foundation of self-awareness and authenticity.

"Most of the shadows of this life are caused by standing in one's own sunshine."
Ralph Waldo Emerson

STRENGTH

Shadow work, when done right, is never easy. And so being able to go successfully undergo this therapy will prove to you all over again that there's really nothing that you cannot conquer as a Black man. This will build up your confidence, self-esteem, and all-round belief in yourself.

FEEL WHOLE

Having an unpleasant part of yourself that you keep in the shadows can make you feel broken at times. It's not only about the pain and the hurt. It also has to do with the knowledge that there's a part of you that you may be ashamed or unwilling to admit to or acknowledge.

Shadow work will help you to understand that despite the feelings of disjointedness and disadvantage that your life's experiences may elicit, not only can you become whole but you have really always been whole. There's nothing broken or damaged about you, irrespective of your past or present. And even if you carry scars from your past, you're are still such a bold and amazing man. Shadow work will help you see this clearly.

RELATIONSHIPS

As your self-awareness heightens through shadow work, you'll learn to trust yourself more. And that trust will extend into improving your relationships.

This is based on the premise that you can't love others if you do not love yourself. Through shadow work, you will come to love and accept every single facet of your being. And by this, your ability to love and respect others, and even validate the struggles of those who have also experienced their own share of pain and hurt in the past will be strengthened.

You will also become better at standing up for yourself. Your heightened self-love will lead to an increased dedication to your self-care. This will embolden you to develop your boundaries and enforce them whenever it comes to your relationships and interactions with others.

"A man who is unconscious of himself acts in a blind, instinctive way and is in addition fooled by all the illusions that arise when he sees everything that he is not conscious of in himself coming to meet him from outside as projections upon his neighbor."

Carl Jung

HEALTHIER HABITS

Your shadow self will often lead you to develop destructive behaviors such as putting yourself down, procrastination, body dysmorphia, addiction, stress eating, and more. You might even begin to justify some of these behaviors as your "coping mechanisms". If not curbed, these behaviors can prove to be ruinous and even fatal to your wellbeing.

Shadow work can help you to nip these behaviors at the bud—the bud being your shadow self. After confronting the reasons for these behaviors, shadow work will then shift your focus to finding healthier and more constructive habits to replace the destructive ones. When you become honest with and open to every aspect of yourself, it becomes a lot easier to be in control of your habits. This way, you can crush the bad ones and substitute them with better ones.

WELLNESS

Suppressing your shadow self can result in all sorts of problems. You may not even realize these problems stem from a repressed side of yourself until you begin to confront that side.

Shadow work will put the control of your wellness back into your hands. The therapy will start at the root causes to address every problem you may be experiencing. It won't just treat your anxiety, chronic fatigue, or any other problem on the surface. It will tackle them from their origins.

"One does not become enlightened by imagining figures of light, but by making the darkness conscious."

Carl Jung

A VOW TO MYSELF

I...,

vow to accept myself.

I vow to let myself live. To live in a way I feel is best for me. To accept all of my flaws, and to put myself and my healing first.

I vow to let myself feel my emotions.

I choose to embrace my wounds.

I vow to give myself a break. To ask for help. To remind myself I am only human.

I look forward to unveiling my shadows.

....

Describe your experience growing up as a black child.

How did your upbringing affect the person you are today?

What are some past traumas that you faced growing up?

How did those traumas affect the man you are today?

_____

_____

_____

_____

_____

_____

_____

_____

_____

_____

_____

_____

_____

_____

_____

_____

_____

_____

_____

_____

_____

_____

_____

What are some lessons you got from your parents about being a child of color in the world?

_____
_____
_____
_____
_____
_____
_____
_____
_____
_____
_____
_____
_____
_____
_____
_____
_____
_____
_____
_____
_____
_____
_____
_____
_____

How did these lessons shape you into the man you are today?

If you could change something about the way you were brought up as a black man, what would you change?

What were you brought up to value in your family?

What kind of household did you grow up in? How did your household affect your life and choices?

Are there any family patterns you fear you are repeating? What are they?

In what ways are you similar to your parents and how they think? In what ways do you hope to be like your parents and not be like your parents?

How are your current values different from those of your upbringing?

Do you think your childhood self would be proud of who you are today? Why is that?

What is something you would tell your younger self if you could?

_____

_____

_____

_____

_____

_____

_____

_____

_____

_____

_____

_____

_____

_____

_____

_____

_____

_____

_____

_____

_____

_____

_____

_____

What's an early childhood memory that has stuck with you into adulthood?

What's your worst childhood memory? How did your parents or guardians respond?

Were you cared for? Were your needs met?

Is there something you deeply regret about your childhood? What is it?

How would you teach your children to be proud of who they are despite their race?

Is there an event in your childhood that brings recurring dreams or nightmares? What happens in them?

Are you happy with where you are in your life?

How do you handle the stress of daily living?

Do you practice self-care? Is there more that you could be doing for your wellbeing?

What makes you feel most valued?

Do you feel like you are sometimes misunderstood?

What misconceptions do people tend to have about black men? List some common stereotypes black men face.

Have these stereotypes ever been directed towards you? If yes, what was your reaction to the situation?

What did you learn about yourself as a person and the world in the process?

Make a list of the forms of discrimination black men face daily on a large scale.

In your words, how does the world see a black man? What are some social struggles that black men face?

Are there obvious solutions to these problems? Propose your solutions to them. If you had the power to change it all in an instant, what would you do?

How do you wish the world would see black men? In a perfect world, what would the black man be seen as?

In what small ways would you bring change to the world?

How do you feel when you see acts of aggression or brutality against black people in the media? How do you cope with these feelings?

What challenges have you had to go through as a black man? What are some challenges you face daily as a black man that doesn't seem like challenges to others?

When it comes to barriers, what barriers have you had to break down?

What negative influences do you encounter as a black man? How do you get rid of those negative vibes?

What do you want people to feel when they are around you?

List some common comments people associate you with.
How do these comments make you feel?

Do you feel lost? Write down what makes you feel this way in your life, your job, your relationship, and so on.

What is your biggest regret and why?

Write a letter to yourself, forgiving yourself for any mistakes you have made.

What are some things you should start saying yes to?

What is one personal achievement that you find difficult to accept?

Are there any emotions that you push away or don't address? Why is that?

Have you always been that way?
What made you do it or start it?

Do your emotions ever get in the way of your rational judgment? How so?

What is a common thing people say when a black man shows emotions?

How do you act when you are angry?

Is it different from the way people acted around you, during your childhood when they were angry as well?

Do you have a lot of rage stored up inside of you? Write out
what made you upset and why you're still angry.

What would you say to the person who has wounded you the most if you could see them and say one thing to them?

Write a forgiveness letter to someone you would like to forgive.

What are your core values? Why did you pick these values as yours to live by?

Imagine you met yourself for the first time. What kind of discussion would you have?

What is something you are afraid of doing? Why are you
scared of it? How deeply are the roots of your fear buried?

What is your deepest, darkest fear? How might you be able to expose yourself to that fear in a safe way?

As a black man, how do you choose to rule and conquer your kingdom, not caring about what people say?

Are you easily influenced by other people's opinions? Do you find it hard to assert your voice?

_____

_____

_____

_____

_____

_____

_____

_____

_____

_____

_____

_____

_____

_____

_____

_____

_____

_____

_____

_____

_____

_____

_____

_____

_____

What dilemmas go through your head often?
What triggers it?

How does your work environment treat you? Does it affect you negatively or positively?

_____

_____

_____

_____

_____

_____

_____

_____

_____

_____

_____

_____

_____

_____

_____

_____

_____

_____

_____

_____

_____

_____

_____

_____

_____

Do you think a change of work environment would be beneficial to your mental health?

Have you ever found yourself in a position where you had to struggle to maintain your identity as a black man? Describe the situation.

How did you find your voice in such a place?

Write down how you believe other people see you, whether positive or negative.

Why do you believe people see you this way?

What do you think are the worst character traits a person can have? When is a time you have demonstrated these traits?

_____

_____

_____

_____

_____

_____

_____

_____

_____

_____

_____

_____

_____

_____

_____

_____

_____

_____

_____

_____

_____

_____

_____

_____

_____

Why was it important to you that you had your opinion heard?

Does mental health matter to you? Why or why not?

For some reason, have you neglected your mental health? Why?

In what ways can you better improve your mental health and wellbeing and be more in touch with yourself?

Do you forgive yourself when you have done something
wrong? When you make mistakes can you move on from
them or do they continue to hurt you?

What are some ways you could be more patient with yourself?

How do you handle stress? What are some things you can do to care for yourself during stressful times?

Have you ever developed an obsessive or unhealthy relationship? How did it happen?

Where did the roots of this relationship start? For example, your childhood, past trauma, events, etc.

Are you happy to be alone in your own company? Do you use other people to fill a void?

Are you 100% yourself around others? Do you put on a
persona or mask to blend into the crowd?
Do you know who you are?

_____

_____

_____

_____

_____

_____

_____

_____

_____

_____

_____

_____

_____

_____

_____

_____

_____

_____

_____

_____

_____

_____

_____

Do you allow yourself to be vulnerable in your romantic relationships? Do you put up walls around yourself and your partner or are you completely open?

Was there a time you opened yourself up to someone and felt rejected? What happened? How has that affected you?

Have you ever had your heart broken?
Write about this time in your life.

Have you ever broken someone else's heart? Was it unintentional or intentional? Write about this.

Which relationships in your life no longer serve you? Which relationships feel obligatory or dutiful?

_____

_____

_____

_____

_____

_____

_____

_____

_____

_____

_____

_____

_____

_____

_____

_____

_____

_____

_____

_____

_____

_____

_____

_____

_____

Consider how you'd feel if you allowed those relationships to dissolve, then think about whether they're worth trying to salvage, and how you may be able to do that.

Pick a core limiting belief that you have and write it down. Why do you think this belief is true about you?

_____

_____

_____

_____

_____

_____

_____

_____

_____

_____

_____

_____

_____

_____

_____

_____

_____

_____

_____

_____

_____

_____

_____

_____

_____

_____

How is this limiting belief stopping you from moving forward?

Make a list of ten self-acceptance affirmations.

How deserving do you truly believe you are?

Is it easy for you to ask for help? Does it make you feel weak or vulnerable? Why do you think this is?

When have you been self-sabotaging or destructive in your life? Examine how you were feeling at the time, and what triggered your behavior.

How are you letting yourself down at this time in your life?
How could you be better to yourself? Consider your health,
finances, relationships, work, etc.

Do you ever find yourself manipulating people in an attempt to protect yourself?

What in your life gives you the most purpose?

The way you spend your time daily will determine how you spend the rest of your life. What are your thoughts on this?

If you could change the world to become the way you want it to be, how would you do it?

In what ways can you start making a change to how black men are seen in the world?

What in your life gives you the most purpose?

Write a thank you letter to yourself, thanking yourself for how far you have come and how you are ready to go further.

What is the meaning of life to you?

What's a question you had as a child that you never got a real answer to? Do you have that answer now?

What is the biggest promise you have ever secretly made to yourself? Have you kept it?

Write a letter to the person you will be 10 years from now. Describe who you want to be, where you want to be, and how you want to be known in great detail.

NOTES & REFLECTIONS

NOTES & REFLECTIONS

NOTES & REFLECTIONS

NOTES & REFLECTIONS

NOTES & REFLECTIONS

NOTES & REFLECTIONS

Made in the USA
Coppell, TX
05 November 2023